Facts About the Earthworm

By Lisa Strattin

© 2021 Lisa Strattin

FREE BOOK

FREE FOR ALL SUBSCRIBERS

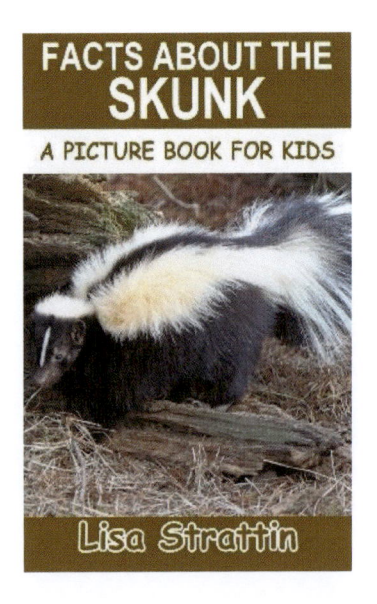

LisaStrattin.com/Subscribe-Here

BOX SET

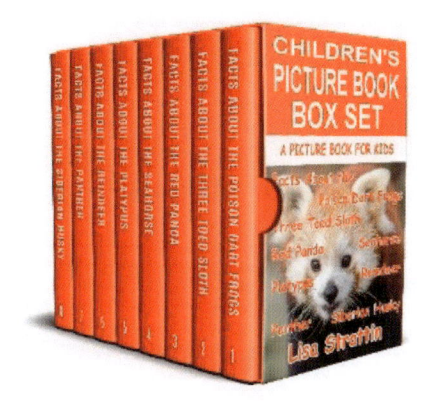

- **FACTS ABOUT THE POISON DART FROGS**
- **FACTS ABOUT THE THREE TOED SLOTH**
  - **FACTS ABOUT THE RED PANDA**
  - **FACTS ABOUT THE SEAHORSE**
  - **FACTS ABOUT THE PLATYPUS**
  - **FACTS ABOUT THE REINDEER**
  - **FACTS ABOUT THE PANTHER**
- **FACTS ABOUT THE SIBERIAN HUSKY**

LisaStrattin.com/BookBundle

Facts for Kids Picture Books by Lisa Strattin

Little Blue Penguin, Vol 92

Chipmunk, Vol 5

Frilled Lizard, Vol 39

Blue and Gold Macaw, Vol 13

Poison Dart Frogs, Vol 50

Blue Tarantula, Vol 115

African Elephants, Vol 8

Amur Leopard, Vol 89

Sabre Tooth Tiger, Vol 167

Baboon, Vol 174

Sign Up for New Release Emails Here

LisaStrattin.com/subscribe-here

All rights reserved. No part of this book may be reproduced by any means whatsoever without the written permission from the author, except brief portions quoted for purpose of review.

All information in this book has been carefully researched and checked for factual accuracy. However, the author and publisher makes no warranty, express or implied, that the information contained herein is appropriate for every individual, situation or purpose and assume no responsibility for errors or omissions. The reader assumes the risk and full responsibility for all actions, and the author will not be held responsible for any loss or damage, whether consequential, incidental, special or otherwise, that may result from the information presented in this book.

All images are free for use or purchased from stock photo sites or royalty free for commercial use.

Some coloring pages might be of the general species due to lack of available images.

I have relied on my own observations as well as many different sources for this book and I have done my best to check facts and give credit where it is due. In the event that any material is used without proper permission, please contact me so that the oversight can be corrected.

COVER IMAGE

https://flickr.com/photos/pfly/128621319

ADDITIONAL IMAGES

https://flickr.com/photos/dodo-bird/477499086

https://flickr.com/photos/goosmurf/3828755105

https://flickr.com/photos/schizoform/93957289

https://flickr.com/photos/schizoform/93957792

https://flickr.com/photos/schizoform/93956444

https://flickr.com/photos/33755808@N08/4633661097

https://flickr.com/photos/regexman/17267840432

https://flickr.com/photos/treegrow/38799468075

https://flickr.com/photos/treegrow/46545838235

https://flickr.com/photos/10413717@N08/6935317800

Contents

INTRODUCTION 9

CHARACTERISTICS 11

APPEARANCE 13

LIFE STAGES 15

LIFE SPAN 17

SIZE 19

HABITAT 21

DIET 23

FRIENDS AND ENEMIES 25

SUITABILITY AS PETS 27

INTRODUCTION

In Ancient Egypt, earthworms were celebrated, and Aristotle called them "the intestines of the Earth." The earthworms hide underground doing so much for our world and we would never even know it!

As the worms tunnel underground, they are mixing the soil so that plants can grow the way they need to! The slime that is on their bodies is full of nitrogen and that nitrogen is very important for plants too! You can find earthworms, also called angleworms, in almost every kind of soil on the planet!

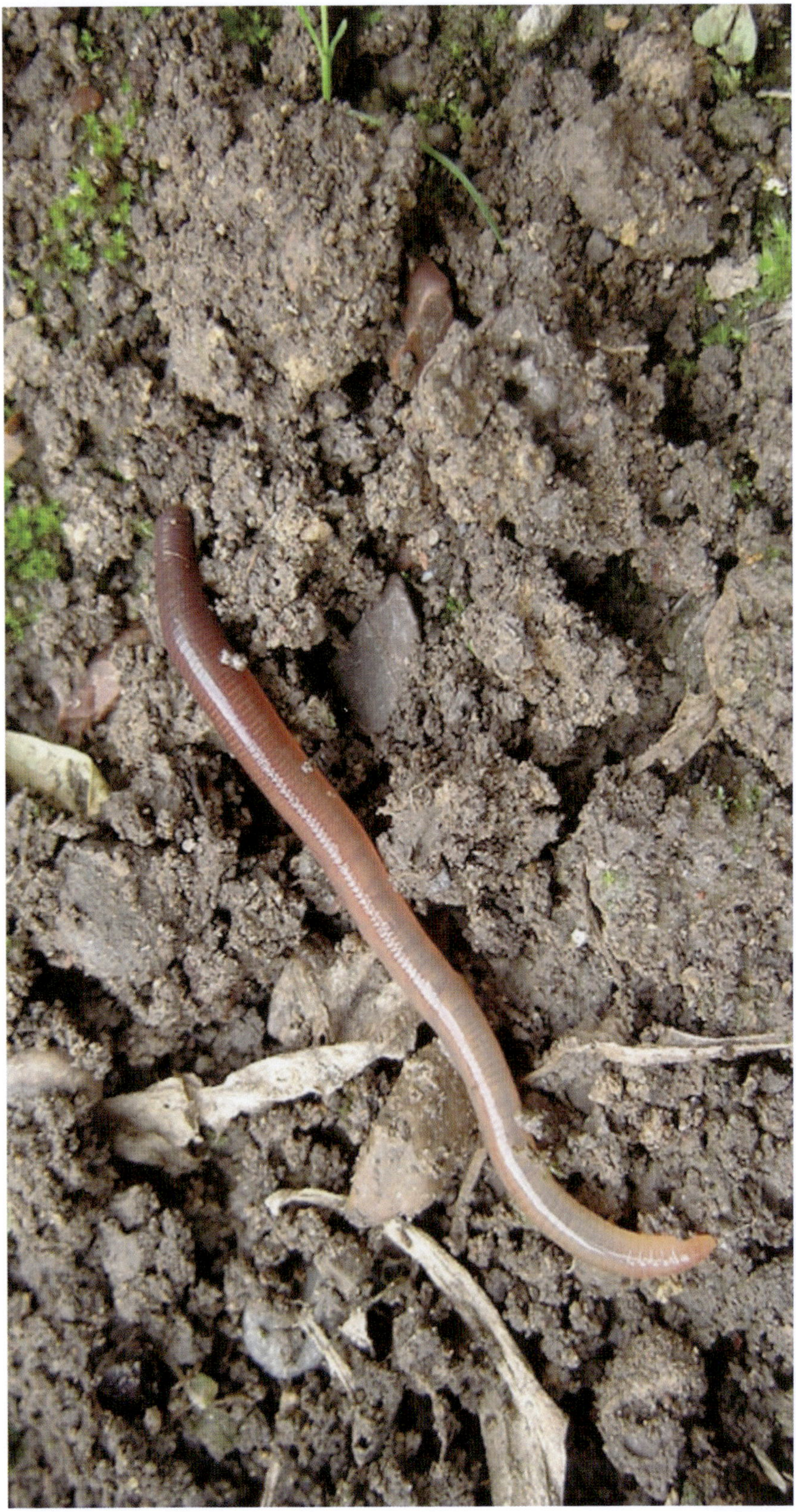

CHARACTERISTICS

Earthworms are soft worms that can be red, brown, or pink and they don't usually get longer than a few inches in the United States. They stay underground during the day and then come to the surface at night to feed. Earthworms cannot see or hear, but they do notice heat and vibrations.

Earthworms are *hermaphrodites*, which means that they have both male and female organs. When the soil gets too hot or too cold, earthworms go through a kind of hibernation called *diapause.* They can become inactive or travel deeper into the soil to protect themselves from the elements. They will stay this way until their soil returns to a more comfortable temperature.

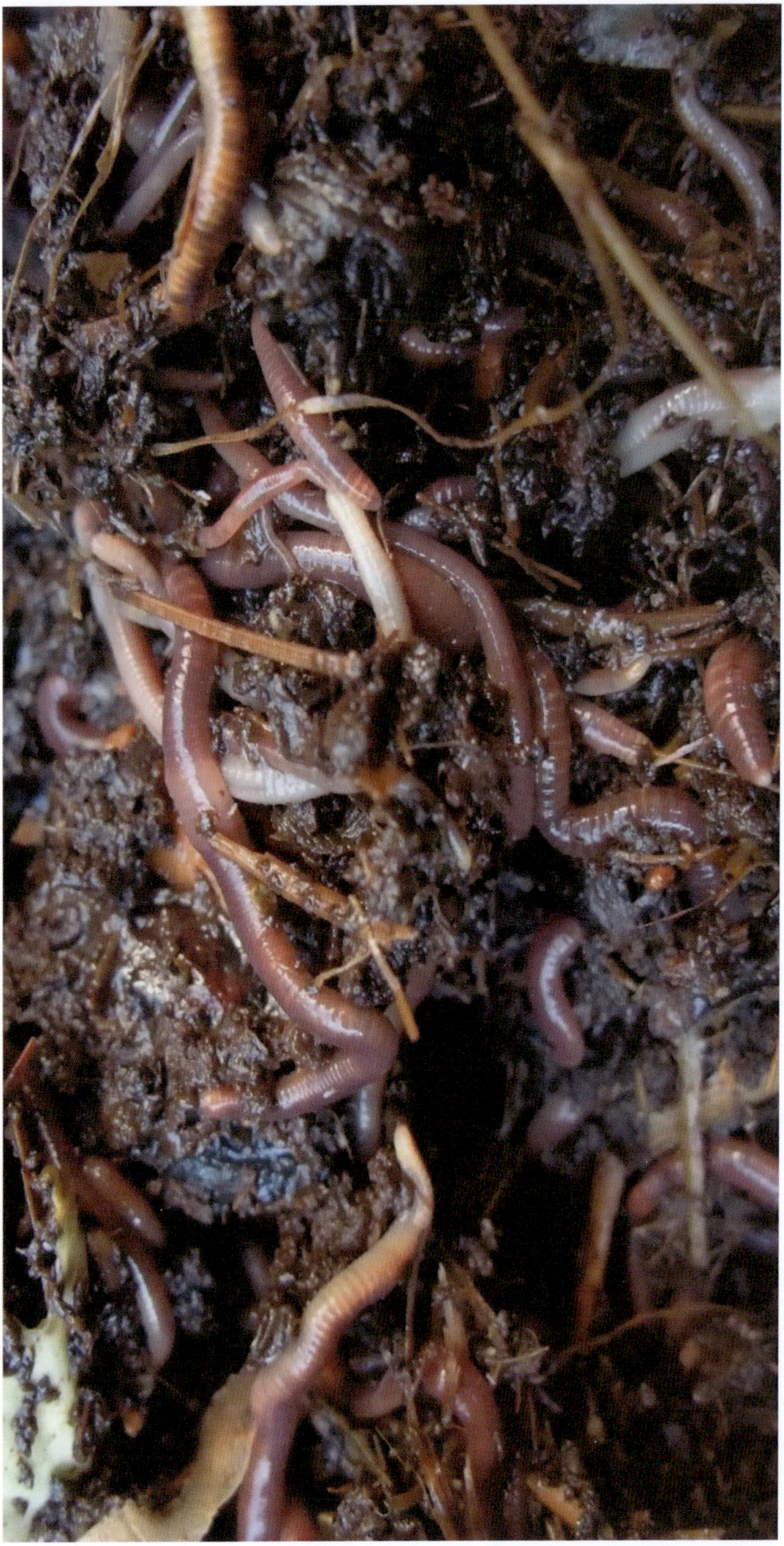

APPEARANCE

Earthworms can come in many different sizes and colors. They are one of the few species that can regrow a body part that is cut off!

They also do not have skeletons – there are no bones in the earthworm at all! Their bodies are made up of soft tissue inside and out. Their bodies are long and cylindrical and are made up of many different segments. Each segment is called an *annuli*. Some species have as many as 150 annuli!

Earthworms have two organs that are similar to the heart in a human's body! Some people might wonder if earthworms have heads and brains – they do! You can tell which end of the worm is its head because it is the end that is usually a lighter color than the other end.

Earthworms do not have ears, noses, or real eyes but they have cells that can detect heat, cold, touch and vibrations! The harsh rays from the sun can kill earthworms so they tend to stay out of the direct sunlight.

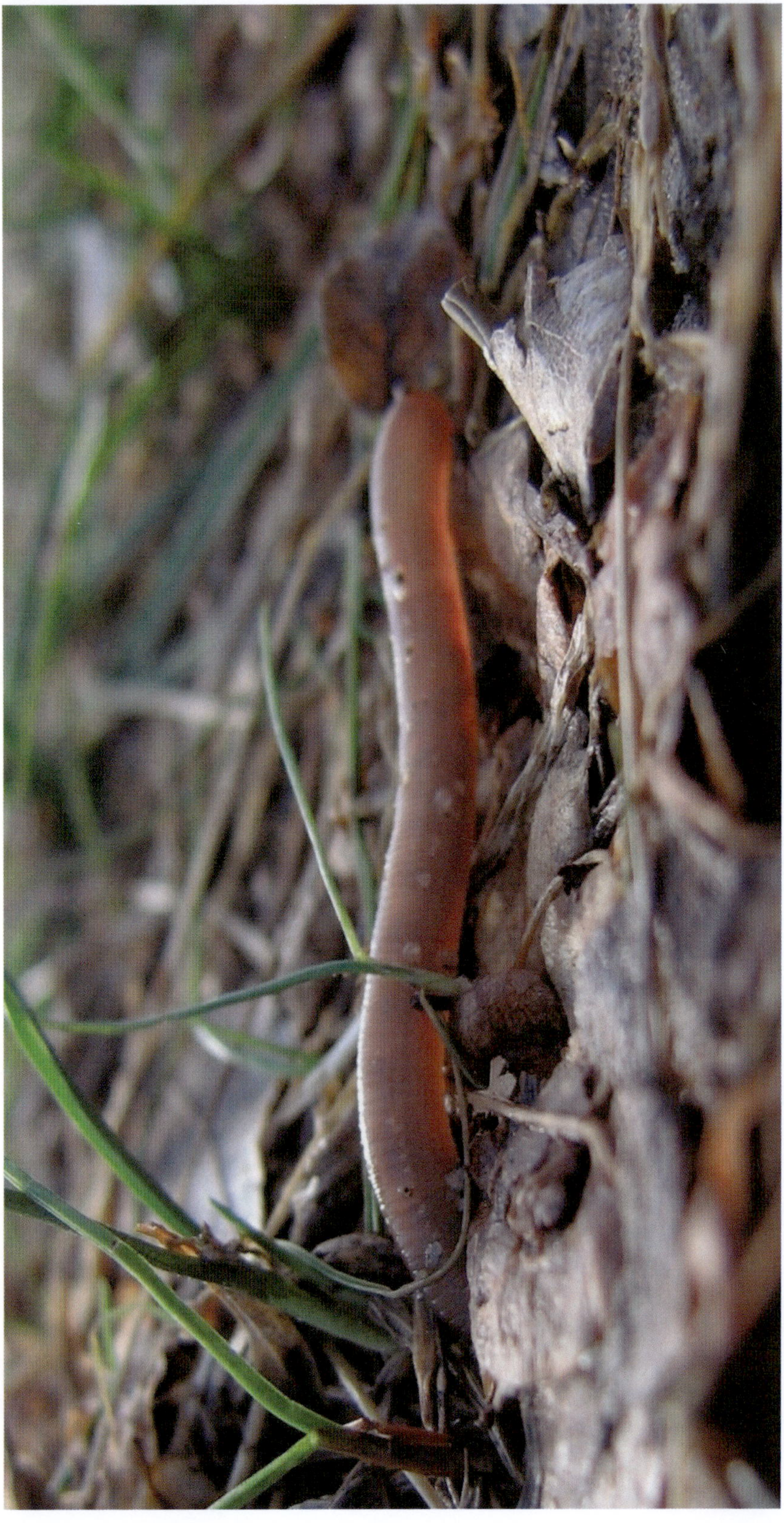

LIFE STAGES

Earthworms are *hermaphrodites* (remember, they are both male and female,) so when it is time to lay eggs, a band of mucous will cover the eggs and this will form the eggs into a cocoon. Some species of earthworm can produce 3 to 80 cocoons a year! These cocoons will be laid directly on the soil. Each cocoon may have up to 20 eggs that are the size of a grain of rice and shaped like a lemon.

Species that live further underground will produce fewer cocoons than those which live closer to the surface.

It can take between three weeks to 5 months for the eggs to hatch. They will stay underground until it is the right temperature for them to hatch. Depending on the species, it takes the babies between 10 weeks to a year to become an adult.

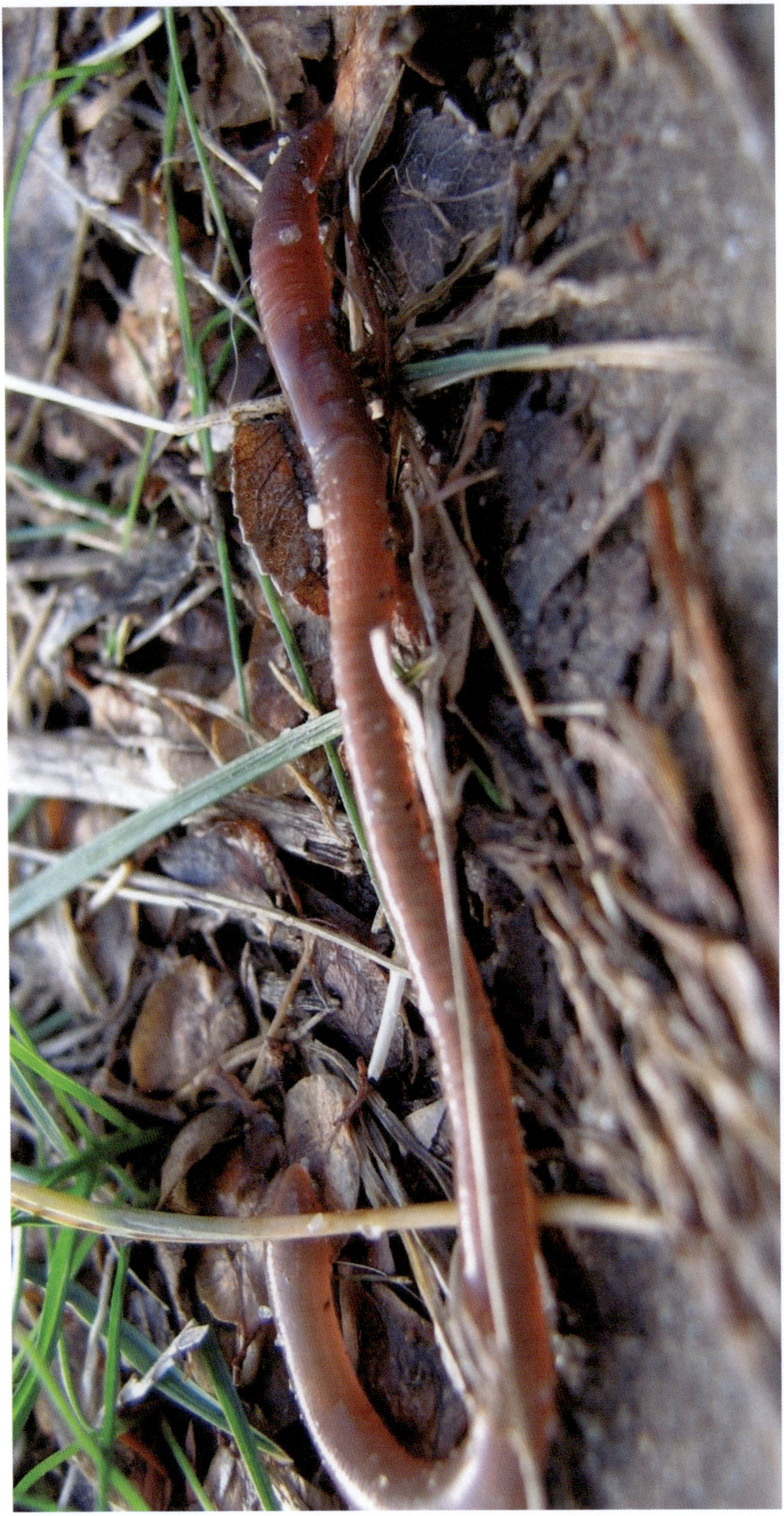

LIFE SPAN

Earthworms are cold blooded creatures, so they survive longer during cooler weather. Excess heat causes problems for them, for example their heart rates will increase, and this can shorten their life spans.

Generally, an earthworm will live about 8 years in the wild, and the ones that live in a garden will live only about 2 years. In a protected and controlled environment, earthworms have been known to live as long as 10 years!

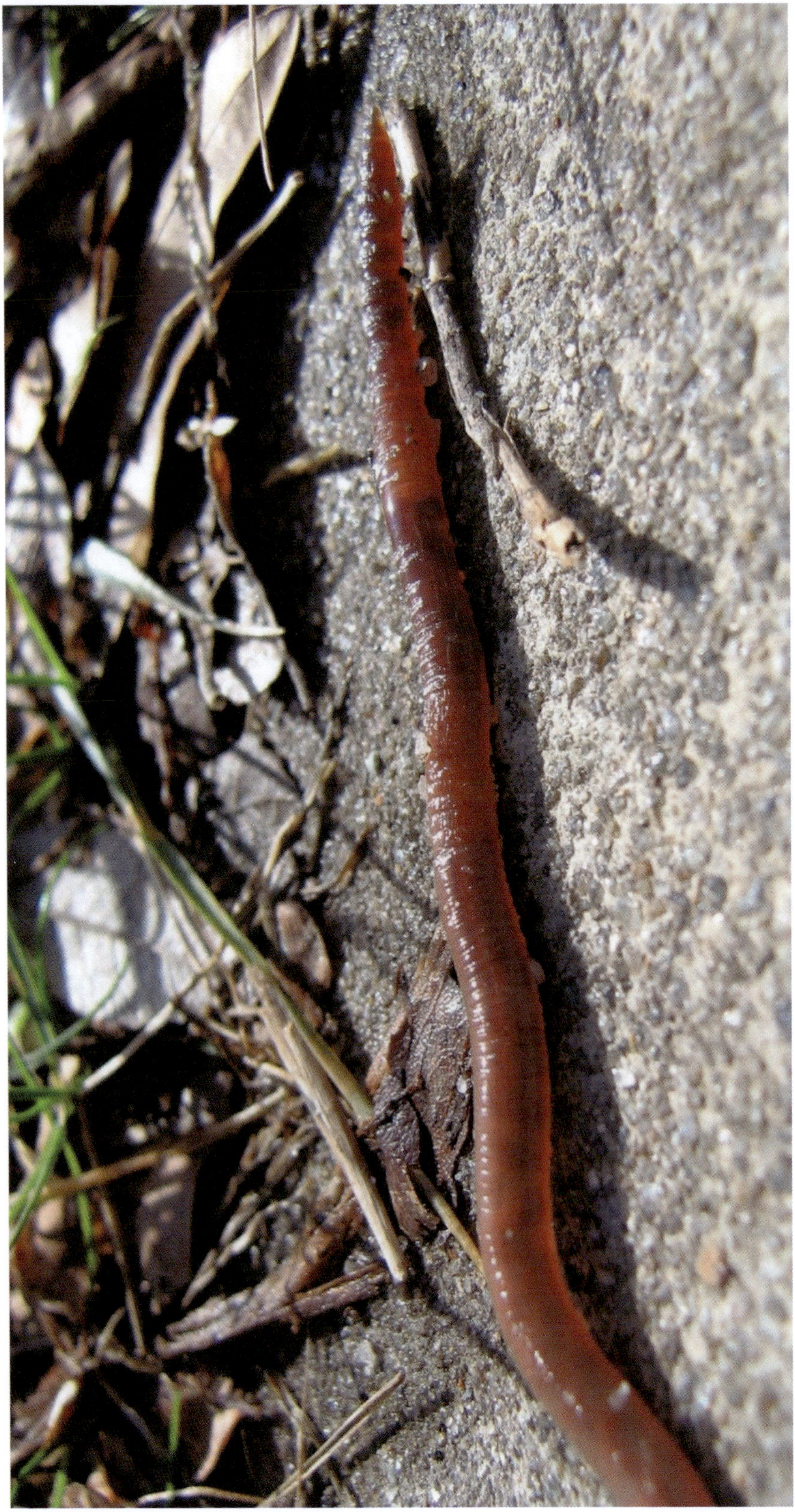

SIZE

Depending on the species, earthworms can be different sizes. Most earthworms that are found here in the United States are only a few inches long, and some are even less than an inch!

In other countries like Australia, they can grow up to 12 feet long and weigh up to 1 ½ pounds! The longest earthworm ever recorded was found in South Africa and was 22 feet long!

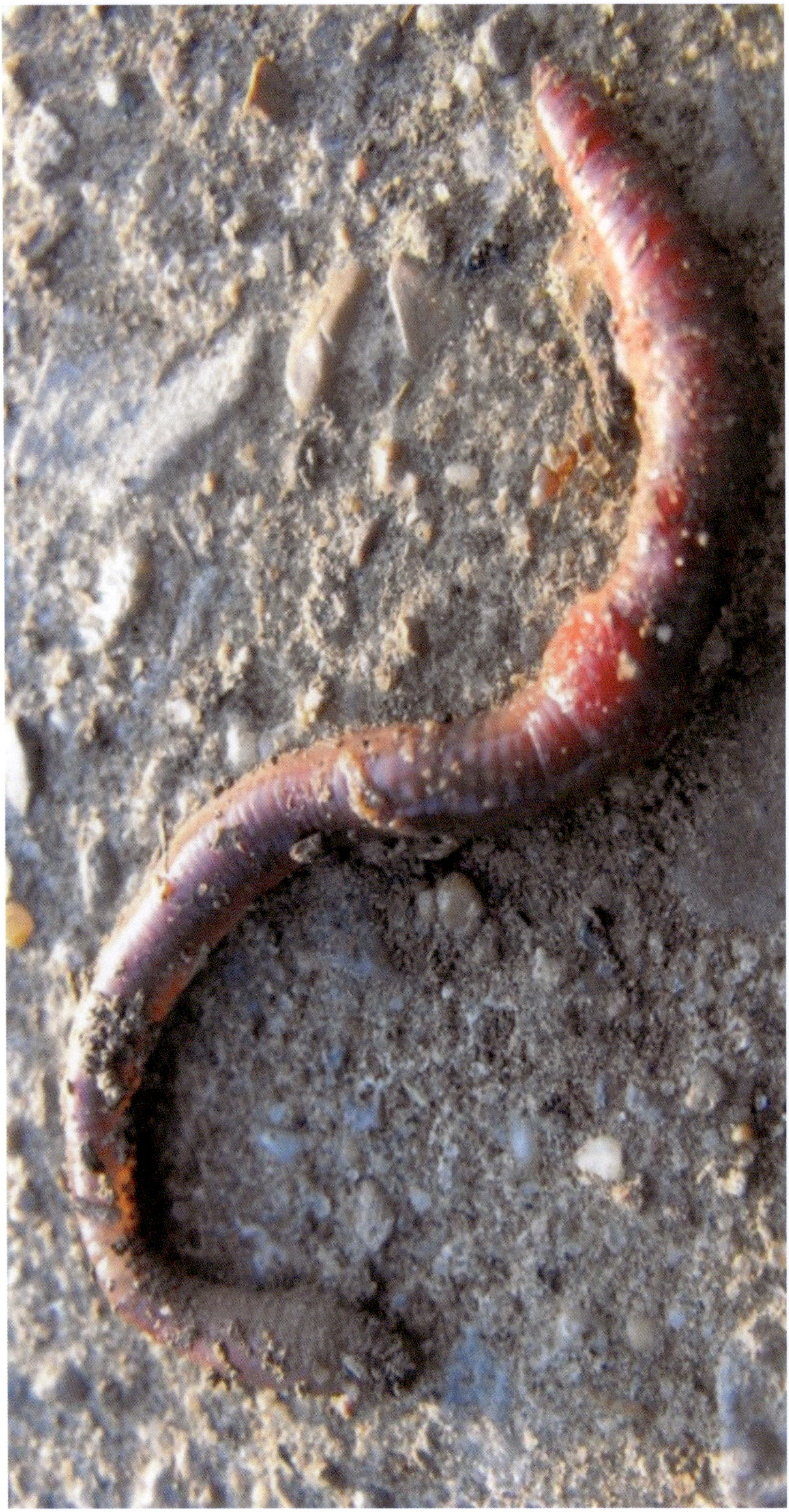

HABITAT

Earthworms love the darkness, damp soil or plant matter. Depending on which species it is, some worms live further into the ground than others. They stay as far out of the direct sunlight as possible because it can kill them.

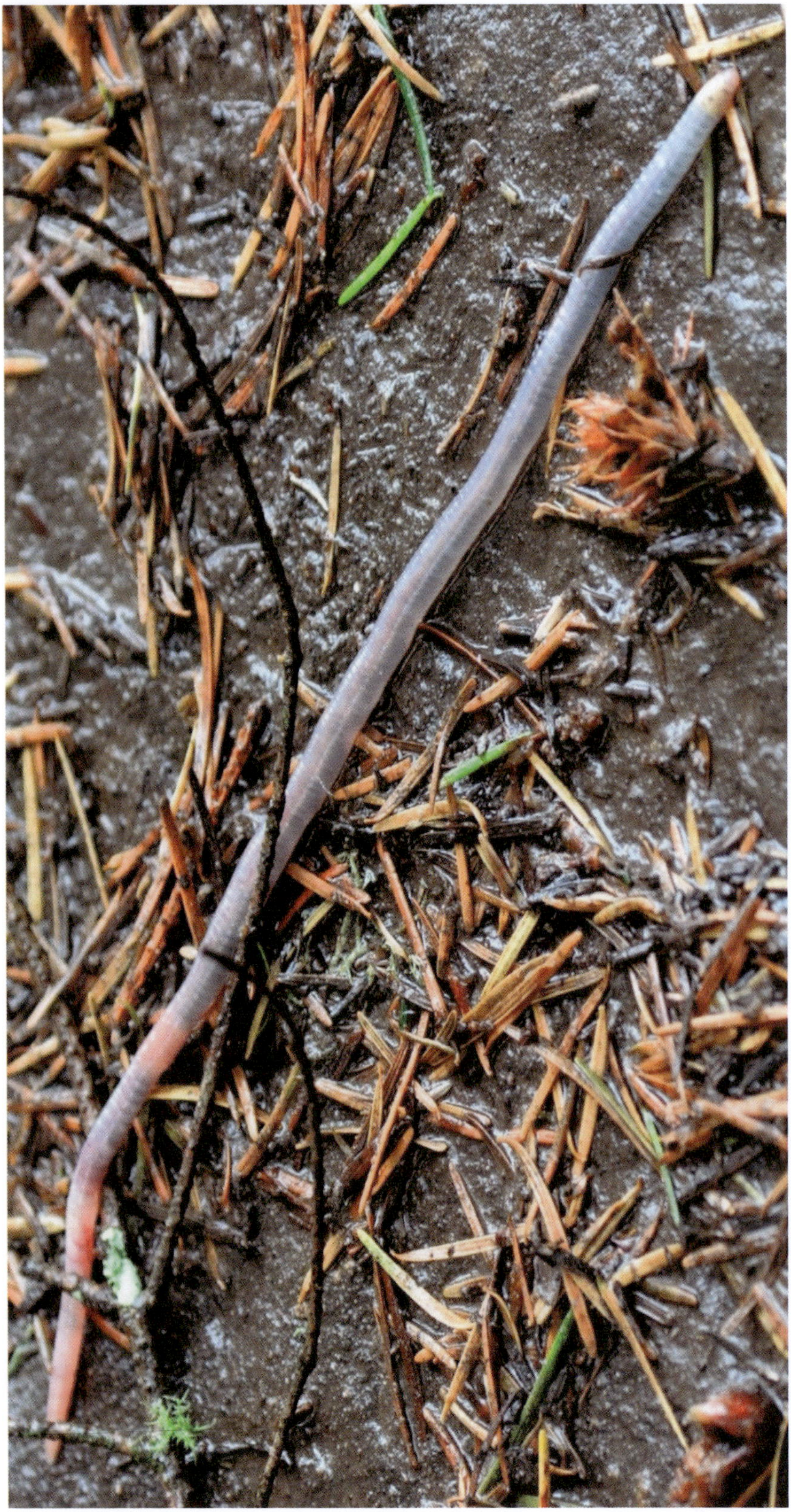

DIET

Earthworms can eat up to half of their body weight in one day! They like to eat the soil and other decaying plant matter that they find as they dig into the ground. The species that live closer to the surface will eat all kinds of plant matter – both decaying and living plants!

They like to snack on decaying roots, leaves, fruits, vegetables, or seeds! The species that live further underground snack on other things like fungus, bacteria, nematodes (microscopic worms,) and any other small organisms that they find down there.

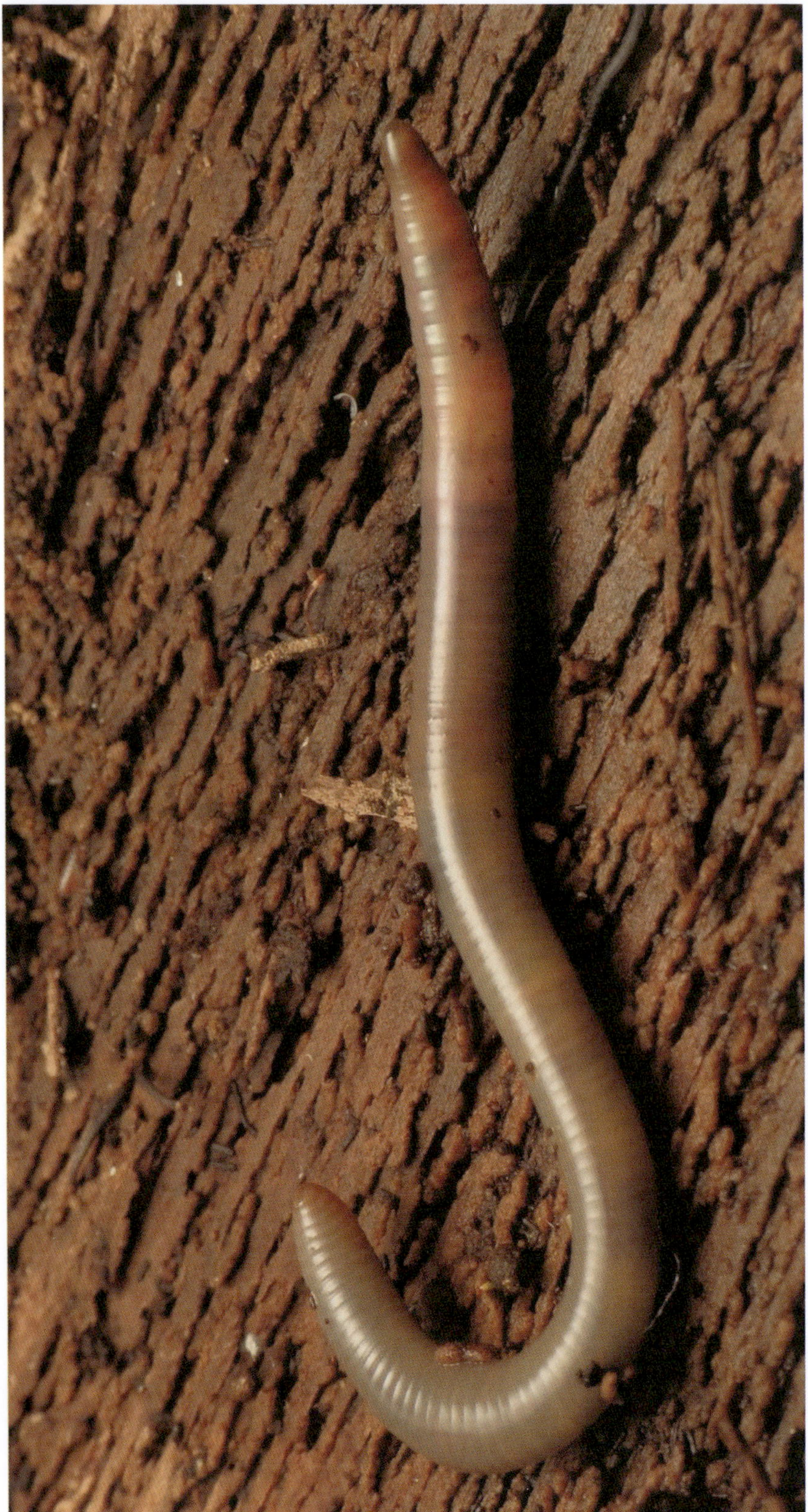

FRIENDS AND ENEMIES

Earthworms have many natural predators. Snakes, birds, toads, rodents, moles, foxes, some kinds of beetles and slugs like to snack on earthworms.

Humans catch the worms to use for bait when fishing!

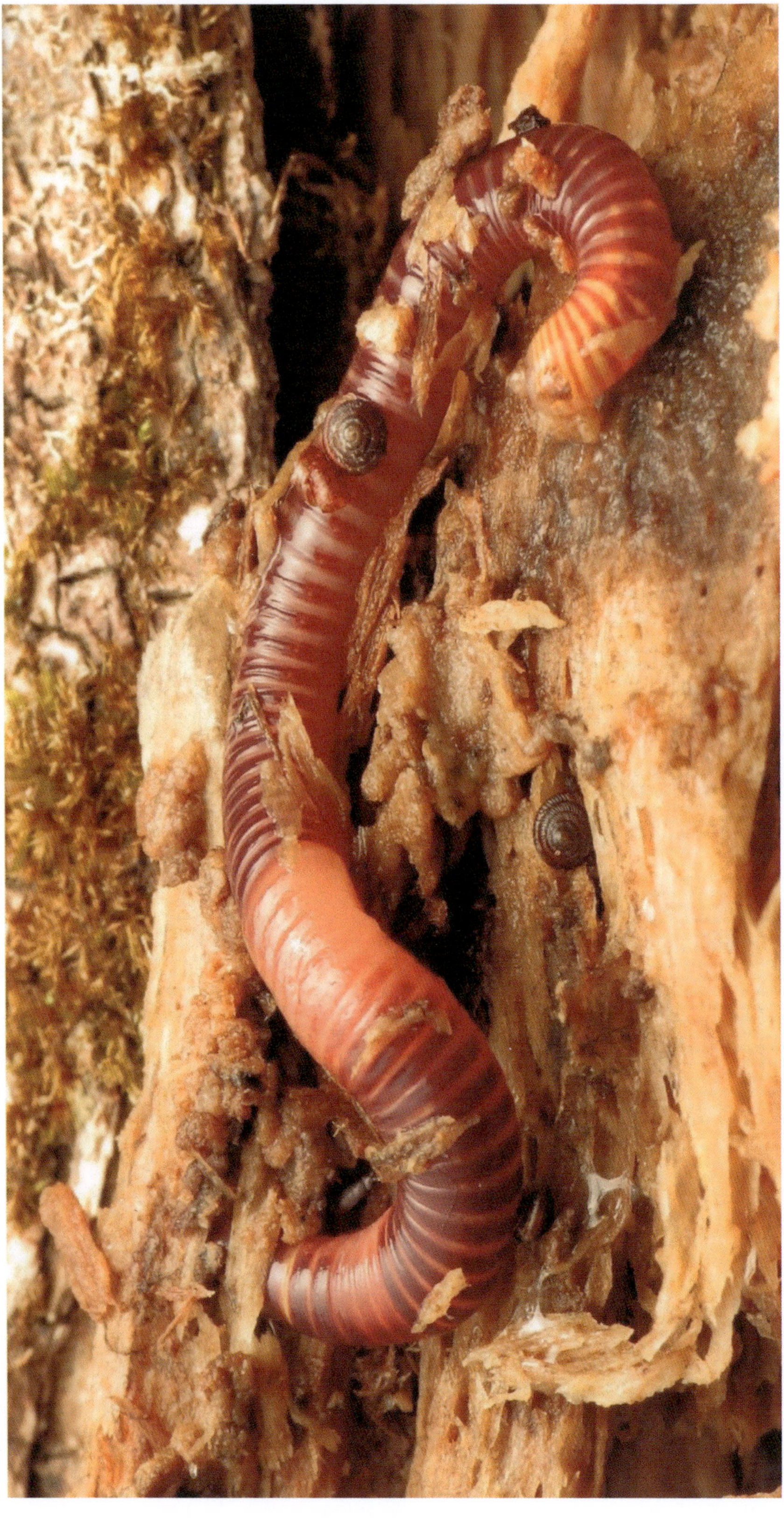

SUITABILITY AS PETS

Earthworms make great pets! They cost very little to get started, and if you have a compost bin on your property then they are extremely helpful! Worms may not be as playful as a puppy or a kitten, but they do not require a lot of care! Worms are not picky about the kind of food they eat. They will eat anything that you have leftover, just don't offer them too much citrus food, they don't like it very much! And best of all, earthworms are great for the environment!

If you want to have earthworms as pets, make sure you have plenty of soil for them to burrow in, an area that is dark and kept at the right temperature. Temperatures that are too hot or too cold are dangerous for earthworms.

A good plan for beginner earthworm owners is to get a plastic bin and poke some holes in it. The holes will let air in so the worms can breathe; and poke some holes on the bottom for drainage. Put some soil in there with the worms and some food, plants especially, and the worms will be happy as can be!

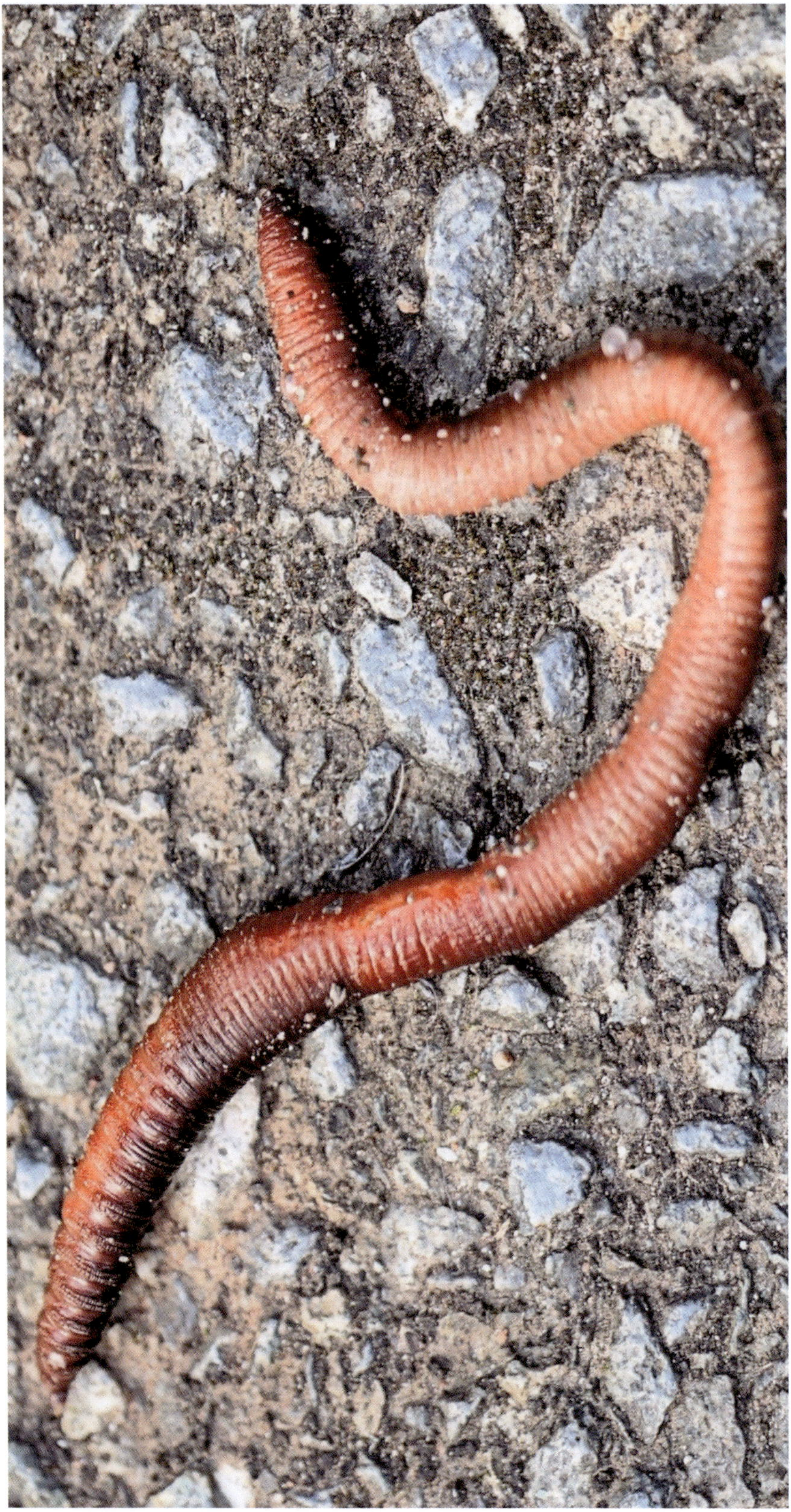

COLOR ME

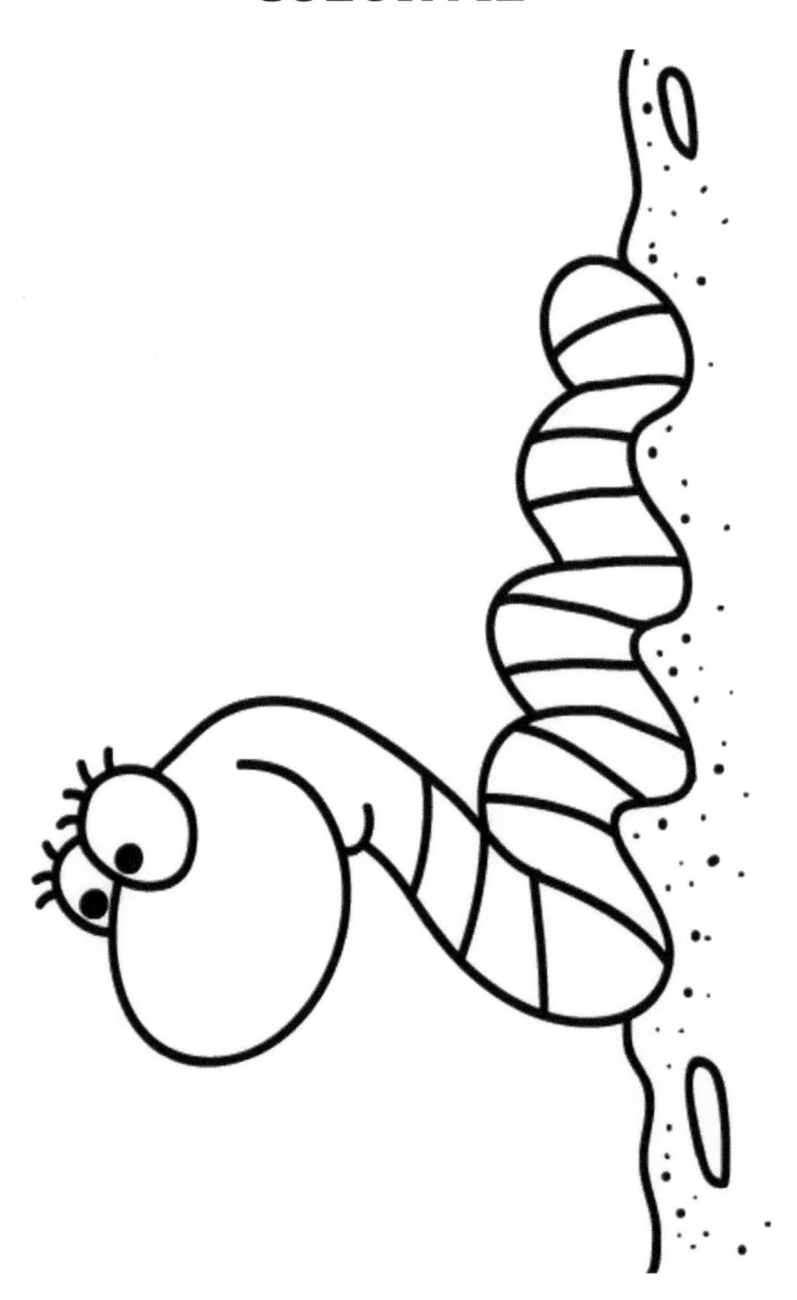

29

COLOR ME

COLOR ME

COLOR ME

COLOR ME

COLOR ME

COLOR ME

COLOR ME

COLOR ME

COLOR ME

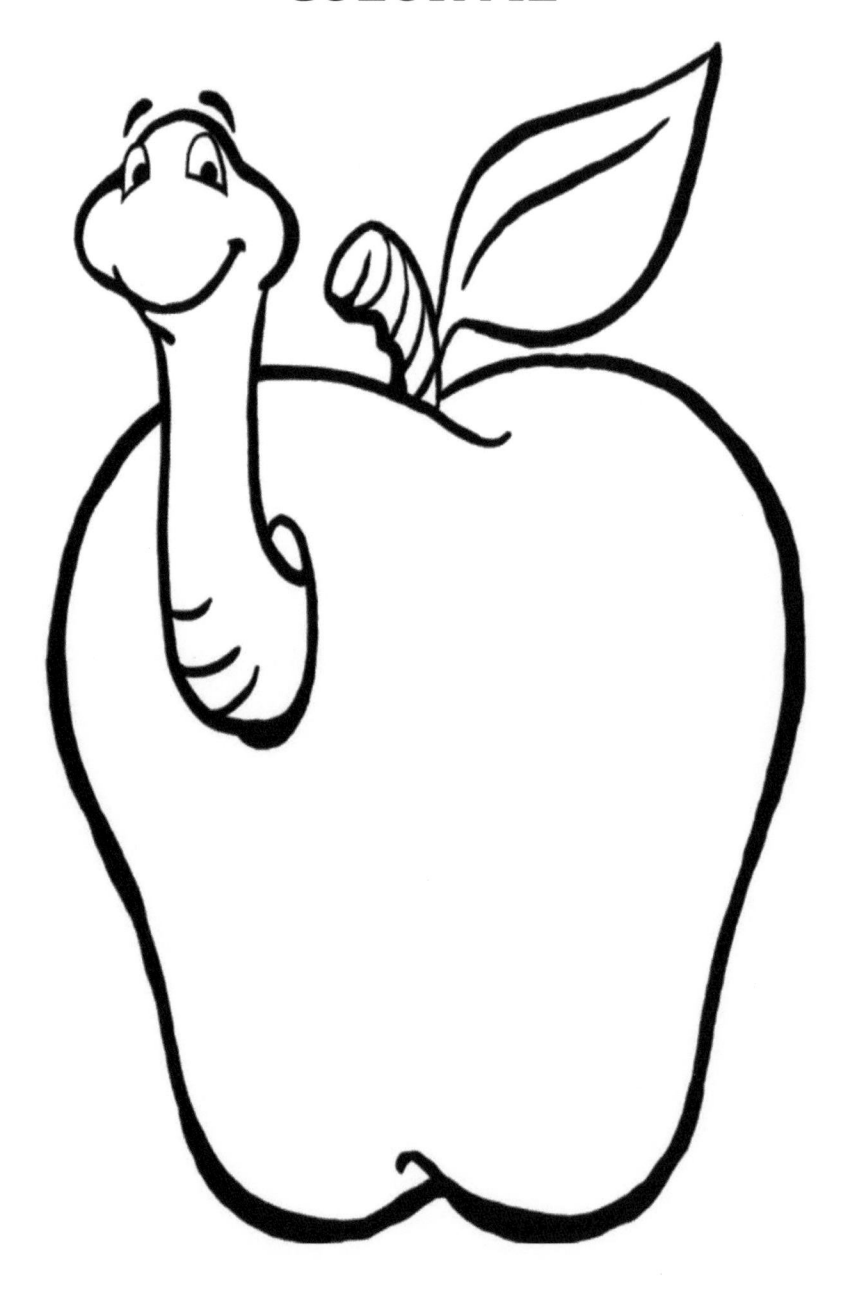

Please leave me a review here:

LisaStrattin.com/Review-Vol-410

For more Kindle Downloads Visit Lisa Strattin Author Page on Amazon Author Central

amazon.com/author/lisastrattin

To see upcoming titles, visit my website at LisaStrattin.com– most books available on Kindle!

LisaStrattin.com

FREE BOOK

FOR ALL SUBSCRIBERS – SIGN UP NOW

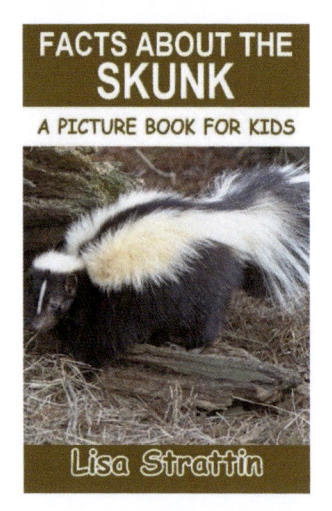

LisaStrattin.com/Subscribe-Here

LisaStrattin.com/Facebook

LisaStrattin.com/Youtube

Printed in Great Britain
by Amazon